25 True Motivational Stories

25 True Motivational Stories

25 True Motivational Stories

Rakesh Kharekar

About the Book

Dear Readers,

The objective of this Motivational book is to highlight how ordinary people inspire us to do more. Many Personalities around the world have done much more than the people mentioned in this book.

We often compare ourselves with famous personalities, Politicians, Businessmen, and Sportsmen. Know this, your destiny is different from those personalities.

You have to walk on your path if you cannot no one else will.

The world is a big stage with Trillions of people following different religions and beliefs. Some are living from hand to mouth and some are living their lives in harmony and still, some do not inculcate the culture of goodness and mental strength among their children.

There is a steep rise in suicide cases, especially among students, who cannot cope with the pressure.

Your small step can save the lives of millions.

About the Author

Rakesh Kharekar is a writer and poet, nemophilist, and aesthete. He lives in the city of dreams – Mumbai. His writing had appeared in Switch magazine in the year 2008 – ***"Impossible is nothing".***

He is an Information Technology specialist and has over 15 years of experience. He is ITIL and Six Sigma certified. He loves to write both fiction and nonfiction stories. His life mantra is – ***"Be honest and positive no matter what".***

CONTENT TABLE

1 | JOKER

This is a true story about myself when I was just a school-going, kid. I am 32year-old now and it wasn't an easy life back then when I was in a boarding school.

Life is tough, well ask any boarder guys. Life away from parents and with no proper food and attention makes it miserable.

One thing is for sure, it toughens you and makes you a better person, teaches you to challenge difficulties, and prepares you to face the world. However, it depends on what you choose to become.

Like any normal kid (14-years-old), I also dreamt of playing Football for our country.

I was a good soccer player because I had very Good Coaches (Mr Faria and Mr Alfonso).

One day after the warm-up session, my coach called us and requested us to form a circle.

It was a daily routine and we were not surprised, that's what coaches usually do.

He called out my name "Rakesh, come here". I was surprised, as he had a very stern voice and it wasn't usual.

"Yes, sir", I said. He said, "stand in the middle of the circle", I stood in the circle.

He said, "he is a Joker". Everybody started laughing at me. I was disappointed, as I was a very hardworking guy and never missed a practice session.

He said, "why are you laughing?". One of the players said, "Sir, you called him a joker".

In response, he said, "I am not talking about a circus joker". I am talking about a Joker, which is used in playing cards".

"Joker is a special card and it can be paired with any other card", in the same way, Rakesh is a special player, as he can play in any position and I want you guys to be like him.

That motivated me and increased my confidence and I haven't looked back since then.

Life is very short, however, throughout your life's journey, you will always meet someone, who will lift you and make you feel special. Make you believe in yourself, push you to walk an extra mile, and encourage you to do more.

The sad part was, I had to quit football to focus on my studies and, it was time to evaluate my financial condition. Today, the time is different and young guys have better opportunities to fulfil their dreams.

If you have a dream, you got to protect it and work hard towards it. I mean, work hard and nothing will stop you. If you believe you can, then you will. It's all in the mind. You may experience roadblocks, discouragement on this journey. Fear not, even life will get tired of upsetting you one day.

Remember, we all are **"jokers"** (Special), we just have to believe in ourselves.

Put your head down and work hard.

Moral: Believe in yourself and you will do wonders.

***

2 | EAGLE

This is not just a motivational story, but a real eye-opener. We sometimes, take things for granted.

We don't even care about others and pass on the judgment, without knowing what that person is going through.

Everyone you meet is carrying some of the other burdens and is tired of this never-ending cycle of poor and Rich.

Some strive too hard but do not get everything they desire and some receive everything, without even trying.

Life has taught me many lessons, but the 3 most important things that I can never forget.

It's hardwired into my mind and soul.

- **Firstly, be a nice human being not great, but nice.**

- **Secondly, respect others and never discriminate.**

- **Thirdly, never give up, no matter what.**

This is a true story of each Eagle. The Discovery channel is very knowledgeable, trust me! I am sure, by the end of this story, you would be glad that you're a human being, who doesn't have to go through such endurance.

Here, we go... This is a story of an Eagle. It can live up to 70 years or more, however, to reach this age, the eagle has to make some hard decisions.

In its 40th year, its long and flexible Talons can no longer grab prey, which serves as food to keep it alive in the jungle. Its long and sharp beak becomes bent. The feathers grow old, thick, and heavy.

The thick and heavy feathers stick to its chest and make it difficult to fly high in the sky. The eagle is left with only two options:

DIE or go through a painful process to stay alive for another 30 years.

The process requires that the eagle fly to any mountain top and sit on its nest.

The eagle knocks its beak against a rock until it plucks it out, no one can imagine the pain the eagle has to go through then the eagle has to wait for a new beak to grow back, and then it will pluck out its Talons.

When its new Talons grow back, the eagle starts plucking its old-aged feathers. This is worth it so that the Eagle can take its famous flight of new life and live for 30 years more. You may wonder….

Why is this painful process needed? Is this only to survive and live another 30 years more? Why not accept fate and surrender?

Well, my friends, it's not about a new life or survival. It's about who you're and what you do with your precious life defines you. God made us unique and have infused all the positive traits to overcome our fears and move ahead in life. Our body is a precious gift of God and we should learn to respect it. Some are not born with a normal body. If you have one, then thank him and make each day of your life count.

Just like an Eagle let go of your ego, negative thoughts, and painful memories. Do not judge, be open and liberal-minded.

Fly, if you fall; try again, just like an EAGLE.

Moral: Don't expect life to be a smooth journey. Have a nerve of steel to face the hurdles and overcome them.

***

3 | IMPOSSIBLE IS NOTHING

This is my story. I was 9 years old and the football season was getting over. Every one of my friends and teammates was getting ready for the Hockey selection before the under/ 10 tournament.

This is still fresh in my mind and now when I look back, I realize how important it was for me not to give up. I had no clue how the Hockey game was played, however, just like everyone, I used to get up early in the morning (5:00 AM) and get ready for Hockey practice. After warming up I had to sit and watch people play and I used to enjoy watching.

Well, you must be wondering. Why did I not play? Hmm…. You won't believe it; however, I did not have Hockey to stick to play a wonderful game of Hockey as I could not afford it. This went on for 2 weeks and one day my coach noticed me. He asked me, "why are you not practicing?" I said, "Sir, I don't have a stick to play the game". He gave me a hockey stick to see how I play. He liked my game and said, "you play well, must practice and you will become a better player". "Come tomorrow and meet me before the practice session and I will arrange a stick for your practice". He also clearly mentioned that "It will be used only for practice".

I was excited and did as I was told. Everything was going well, however, the practice was not enough to get selected for an U/10 team. I had to find a way to practice during my leisure time. The question was, "who can lend me a Hockey stick for practice". My Practice Hockey stick was only meant for the morning practice session.

I was lucky as I had an elder brother Rajesh Kharekar, who understood the situation and borrowed a stick from his friend for practice during my leisure time. Everything was going as per plan and the practice made me better and better each day.

I was selected to represent my school and it was time to deliver.

We did well to reach third place and to my surprise, I was nominated Man of the match and an outstanding player of the tournament and the prize was a Hockey Stick.

I never expected such a feat even though there were many good players on my team. I still remember my friend saying a guy without a Hockey stick has been named an Outstanding player of the tournament… only because he wanted to be the best. I was also awarded for writing this article in one of the magazines. Well, there are many inspiring true stories, however, this is no less than a movie.

My objective is to inspire people who can make it big in life. Tough situations are important to shape you and make you tough and prepare you to face any situations in life. Mental strength is important to let go of bad experiences and learn from them. Good memories let you get inspired and achieve your dreams.

Impossible is nothing only if you do not have an impossible word in your dictionary.

Things to remember

- **There is no substitute for hard work.**
- **Do what you feel is good.**
- **You're your competition and try to be better than you were yesterday.**

Moral: Hard work doesn't require any miracle; it comes to us naturally.

***

4 | EVERYTHING HAPPENS FOR A REASON

Does everything happen for a reason? Some may agree and some may agree to disagree. To be honest, not everything happens for a reason. However, my experience cannot deny the fact that "Everything happens for a reason"

I was working with one of the Multinational companies back in 2013 and I used to commute via public transport. The railway is the backbone of Mumbai city as lakhs of people commute by train. As usual, I was walking towards the station.

I noticed a pile of plastic items lying on the footpath to attract buyers. It works well for hawkers to advertise their products and earn good money.

As I was walking on the road and approaching a footpath, I suddenly noticed the pile of plastic items slowly crumbling. I did not pay much attention. The moment I climbed the footpath as it had already fallen. I felt bad I was in a position to save it from falling and that made me guilty for not reacting. To my luck, nothing happened to the goods, as it was made up of tough plastics and I was glad and hawker did not incur any loss.

I reached the platform to board the train, however, I could not stop thinking about it even though no damage was done. A loud announcement grabbed my attention and it was intimated about the arrival of the fast train on platform no.1; a guy next to me was busy on a phone call and was walking at the edge of the platform. Again, the travellers were informed about the arrival of the fast train on platform no.1 in 3 languages, the guy next to me was still walking near the edge of the platform.

I was still thinking about my incident and walked past the guy next to me, as I was about to cross; I saw a train approaching the platform and the man was still on his phone not bothered about the situation.

Something happened, which forced me to pull the man from the edge of the platform towards safety, the train passed by like a trace of a bullet. I saved that man's life. Yes, I did, then I realized how important it was for me to be vigilant.

Saving that man's life gave me great relief and made me realize that saving plastic goods was not planned for me, God had bigger goals and tasks. This incident made me wonder that whatever happens, it happens for the best or a reason. You either learn from it or run from it.

God always has plans for us and his goals are far greater than ours.

Life is all about giving, it's an altruistic act of helping one another even our enemy. Life is all about turning an unfriendly environment to your advantage. Finding happiness in sadness and hope in worries.

Life may not be like a bed of roses or a walk in a park. Life is more than that. It makes us stronger, wiser, and smarter with experiences and incidents. Tough life can shape you and mould you to become a person who never gives up no matter what and that's what makes us unique.

We all are different and hence we should respect our differences and keep moving forward. Why? Because everything happens for a reason and you're born to do great things!

God's plan is far greater than ours

Moral: Life can be a friend, foe, and a teacher; treat it the way you would like to be treated.

***

5 | JOURNEY FOR A SURVIVAL

"Journey for survival" is about my struggle in my school days.

I was in 10th Standard and was struggling with the financial

condition.

I had a month to prepare for my S.S.C. exam and it was getting tougher and tougher to survive day by day. Had to take a loan from someone, though my Dad was alive and was living happily.

Since I had no relatives in Mumbai, it was difficult to ask for money from others. Friends had the same problem. I started catering service in a 5 Star hotel, however, that was not enough as I had to prepare for my S.S.C. and I couldn't take a risk of failing.

Finally, I decided to travel and visit my dad and take a loan of Rs.1000. This was important for education and survival. I booked a train ticket from Dadar station. In the meanwhile, my brother was working hard as we were living from hand to mouth.

Reached the station at night and boarded the train. It was usually crowded and literally standing on one foot for an hour. It was congested and packed. Slowly and steadily, reached the seat.

Had only Rs.15 in my wallet. It was a big risk; however, I had no choice. The train stopped at one of the stations and the coolie approached me and demanded Rs.10 to reserve a seat for me. I gladly gave it to him.

Trained stopped at another station after an hour. 1 more coolie marched towards me and pushed me away and gave my seat to another man. I was not really in a position to fight back.

People around me supported me and somehow, I got a seat. Oh! With a sigh of relief, I thanked God.

Occupied my seat. My focus was on collecting money and exam preparation. Even on the crowded train, I could not take my eyes off the book. One of the gentlemen noticed and asked me about my whereabouts. Told him that I am travelling to visit my dad and preparing for my S.S.C. exam. He was a judge in one of the courts and was transferred to one of the states in India. I congratulated him and started my studies.

While memorizing, I overheard about the train schedule and destination information. Someone just said Punjab is very far.

"Did I hear that correct", I
thought about it.

Slowly my heartbeat increased and had to face my worst fear. I was on the wrong train, which was travelling to Punjab state and I wanted to travel to Khamgaon within Maharashtra State.

My heart sank and with a soft voice, I asked my co-passenger, "is this train journeying to Khamgaon"?. He said, "No, this is travelling to Punjab".

I had no clue and did not know what to do next. I gathered some courage and asked for an alternate solution. One guy said, "you can get down at Wardha station and catch another express train to Nandura". Finally, a relief. Once again got down to the Wardha station and boarded the train to Nandura, which was 17 – 19Km. away from Khamgaon.

Reached Nandura station at 5:30 A.M. and was surprised to see a Ticket conductor, I had a ticket and showed it to the conductor, and walked out of the station. I was still not home, remember Khamgaon is 17- 19Km. Away from Nandura.

Since I had only Rs.5 in my wallet, I could not board the Bus to reach my dad's hometown. I was short by Rs.3 and thought someone could help me, Boarded the bus.

As the conductor was closing into my seat, my blood ran cold. I politely asked my neighbour if he can help me with

Rs.3, he obliged and I thanked him with a genuine smile before leaving the bus. One after another problem, I was almost close to the house, however, still far by 3 Km. I politely asked a rickshaw driver to reach me at my house and also told him that I have no money, however, I'll pay him once I reach; he agreed. He was an interesting guy and kept me entertained throughout the journey as it was freezing outside. I reached home, gave the man Rs.10, and thanked him for his generosity.

I can never forget this journey as it was about survival, tenacity, and mental strength. All these tough times not only made me down to earth also made me believe in one thing, if you're focused and do the right thing then nobody can stop you, even God will help you to achieve the impossible. At every stage, I was helped by someone that cannot be a coincidence. One thing is for sure, no matter where we are, God is always there to help us when we're in need, he helps those who help themselves.

You may visit a temple, church, or mosque. You find people are gentle and very cooperative, however, the same people may not be so gentle outside the holy places. Why is that? All I can say is that if you can find God in the holy places then you can also find him outside, God lives everywhere, he lives in us and we live in him.

Dear readers, always respect the people around you, because no one is small or big. Our thoughts and actions make us who we are.

My journey has taught me to believe in humans, the importance of helping one another; It's the greatest gift you can give to the needy.

Never fear to help others, that's the true meaning of life.

"Love thy neighbour as thy self", is what life is all about caring for one another and living life to the fullest, and fulfilling the purpose of our life.

"Believe in yourself and you will do just fine"

Moral: Believe in yourself and trust in the Almighty, you will never be lost.

***

6 | SCHOOL RACE

I was in a 3rd standard and just like any other kid; I too was excited to participate in the school sports. I and my friend wanted to participate in a dual race due to our excellent coordination. We knew without proper coordination and pace, it was difficult to win the dual race.

The dual race rule is simple, the left leg of one player is tied with rope to the right leg of the other player. They're required to finish the race together. Trust me, it's tough if you do not keep up with the pace of your partner.

My friend and I did well during the practice race; however, competing in such a competition always involves the risk of falling and a higher risk of a stampede.

Small kids are fearless and do not think before reacting hence parents are always requested to accompany them. Unfortunately, my parents could not come, and being a boarding boy, it was difficult to invite parents due to various rules and restrictions. We're accompanied by our teachers to look after us.

The stage was set for the big occasion. The ground was roaring with the names of their favourite runners, parents encouraging the children's names. Teachers motivate the students and try their best to control the crowd. It wasn't a big ground; however, sufficient for the small children to feel proud and prove themselves to their parents and teachers. I and my friend were least bothered and were roaming around nothing thinking about winning or losing the race. My friend asked me "what prize is awarded to the winner?"

I laughed astonishingly, even though we had a chance to come out as the winner. I said, "I am not aware of it" "maybe a tiffin box or a box of chocolate, I guess". I was surprised as he did not feel discomfiture.

He was totally in a different world. I wish I could say the same thing about myself; however, I was more concerned about winning the race.

Winning and losing don't matter when you get mature; however, a small kid doesn't understand due to limited knowledge and understanding.

The race started, I and my friend were standing on track 3, overly conscious about giving all out on the race track. Roped was tied to our legs and the race started. We ran and almost reached the finish line, then all of a sudden, I and my friend fell and he became unconscious. We were 5 steps away from the finish line and the rest of the participants were struggling in the mid half of the track. I had no choice but to drag him to the finishing line. The moment was amazing as who could have thought about dragging your partner to reach the finishing line as it was a dual race and both partners are supposed to finish the race together.

Few participants raised questions and demanded disqualification; however, the principal said, "the rule doesn't say you cannot fall, it says to finish the race with your partner", "the boy dragged his friend to the finishing line and did not give up". "If I do not encourage him now, he will never understand the meaning of tenacity".

We were jubilant for finishing the race as the winner.

I learned many things that day

- **Never give up.**
- **There is no substitute for hard work.**
- **Success has no age; however, we learn more from failure.**
- **Always motivate children to give their best in everything they do.**

Moral: Success should keep us focused and failure, humble.

***

7 | A BEGGAR

This story is about a beggar, who used to stay on the street near my society.

I do not wish to use this word to address a person in need; however, it's a demand of this true story. He used to beg for alms, live, and sleep on the street. I used to wonder, why on earth does he beg? As he was mentally and physically fit and could have earned money without begging.

As a college-going student, I had many things to worry about me and hence did not bother him. One day while coming from college; I noticed him feeding a dog, which reminded me of a very famous proverb "One act of kindness at a time". I was perplexed by his behaviour; however, happy with his generosity for an animal. Being an animal lover myself, I understood his benign gesture.

This went on for months. Days turned into months, months turned into years. This was a daily mundane for him and a daily sight for me. One day a beggar fell ill, though he could walk around and did not give any sign of illness to others. A dog became his good friend and they both used to have a great time enjoying each other's company. The condition of the beggar was getting worst day by day, we came to know about it later. He could not beg and was bedridden.

Other beggars helped him with his daily needs; however, it wasn't sufficient. While returning from college, I thought of buying food for the beggar. When I came close to the beggar's tent; I saw a dog carrying a chapatti for his master. I still remember the beautiful sight of a friendship.

All these years, his master was feeding him and when the master fell ill; Dog used to feed him, even though it wasn't feasible for the poor animal.

My heart sank and I left the food near the beggar's tent. This was a beautiful sight of a friendship; how often we forget that, we're here to love, serve, make friends and help one another.

An animal thought me a great lesson that day. No matter how small or big you're, there is always room for generosity for others. As a human how can we forget that?

I realized that, if you want to do something for someone, you go the extra mile to help the person in need. With small sacrifices, we can win the heart of others and probably change or touch the lives of other people.

Life is all about doing the right thing and living with principles.

Appreciate what we have and enjoy while we can as no one is permanent on this planet called 'Earth'.

We all have to go one day from this world and the answer to the almighty. Do not help others in the context so you're blessed, help so you achieve inner peace. The satisfaction of helping others is sweet and quite amazing. Some so many people help others willingly with no expectations.

This story not only teaches us to help others; also, to love ourselves. If you cannot love yourself then how can you love others? Do not be hard on yourself. Always remember, whatever happens, happens for the best and there is no point in thinking about the things you cannot change. Instead, move on and spread happiness through your work.

"A friend is one who not only helps you but also brings the best out of you."

Moral: A friend in need is a friend indeed.

***

8 | LOYALTY

One of my friends was working as a salesman for one of the brand companies. The stipend was less; however, worth every effort to represent that brand of car. He was qualified; however, could not get a job as per his qualification. He thought of working as a sales representative in the interim.

An interesting incident happened to him. You may call it a stroke of luck or fate, I'll leave that up to you. He was called to an exhibition to represent his company's car; many other salesmen were also present to represent their company's branded cars. He had to go through rigorous training to understand the features and important specifications of the car. He worked hard and finally got ready for the final day.

One of the buyers from the crowd approached him and showed little interest in the car and later started comparing his car to other brands. He was bombarded with tough and many provoking questions, such as, "How is your car different from others?" "What's the mileage?" "why is it costly?".

My friend was calm and cool and give his best to tactfully handle a tough customer. He kept elaborating on the features and how it's different from other branded cars; why he should buy his car and why his company is different from the competitors.

He always had a smile and knew how to deal with tough and tricky situations. The tough customer was loud and kept arguing and during the explanation, my friend realized that customer is no ordinary guy as he was aware of all the features, such as the number of the valve, how often the oil is changed, the capacity of the engine, etc.

He was a little tense; however, did not reveal the nervousness on his face during the debate. The buyer kept arguing and testing his patience.

My friend kept smiling, neither of them were ready to give up. Finally, a buyer asked him, "why do praise the car of your company even when you know there are better cars in the exhibition?". He replied, "I work for the company and it's my responsibility to be loyal and stick to my words as they". "Doesn't matter how a person or a company treat you, you should always be loyal, because at the end of the day; it's what you choose to be and I am not deceitful". The buyer was happy and asked him to come with him. My friend was baffled and asked, "where to?". "To my office", he replied and cunningly smiled and said, "I am the Marketing Director of your company".

My friend was offered a Sr. Marketing manager post and he never looked back since then.

This story teaches us many things, especially about loyalty, positive attitude, tenacity, mental strength, and last but not least patience.

He tactfully dealt with the buyer and never even once replied rudely.

Life is all about converting negative things to positive. Only the weak give up, the strong don't show their backs even when they know that they have no chance of winning.

If we all give our cent per cent in our daily lives; we can never be defeated. We say, "It's all in the mind", so true. You become what you think and become someone, who has to be that person. We cannot fathom someone's loyalty; however, a person's behaviour speaks about his attitude.

"Right attitude is a great attitude."

Moral: A loyal person is invincible.

***

9 | FAILURE

This story is about my childhood friend – **Agnelo Cardoz**; he was an average student just like any other boarding boy. He had a keen interest in sports and not in study.

Time passed by and he kept failing every alternate year. The boarding in charge was disappointed with his effort and did their best to motivate him to be better in his studies; however, nothing worked.

Since I was very close to him; had advised him many times about the importance of studies and how it affects our professional and personal lives. He was a moody soul and a dreamer and things did not go well with him his studies. Even though he was disinterested in studies; he was a hardworking guy, kind-hearted, and always had a genuine smile.

Somehow, he cleared his S.S.C. after a setback. His father passed away just when he was appearing for his 9th standard exam. I still remember that day; a nightmare for a dear friend; however, I had to be strong to console him.

Things changed as he started taking responsibility. He was eager to leave the boarding and join the workforce. As he wanted to earn money and stand for himself, which was tough; however, not impossible.

He worked in a catering job and did a part-time job in a hotel as a receptionist. Though he was living from hand to mouth, he never complained. Kept doing what was right; did not give up in tough situations.

Despite working hard, he was living hand to mouth and really had no option to seek help; as I too was struggling with my life; I could not do much for him. A year passed by, his financial condition kept improving. He became more confident, reliable and developed a very strong personality.

One fine day, my brother asked him to apply to a media channel and try his luck as he was suitable for the job. He felt discomfiture and skipped the interview. As soon as my brother came to know about it. He went to his place and scolded him to try again. This time he had no option as he was accompanied by my big brother. His name was called for a face-to-face interview; he was nervous but gathered all his energy to give one last shot.

He came out of the cabin after 20 min and was very excited as he was offered the job and his pay hike was doubled. He was on cloud nine and could not believe his luck. Today he is working with a reputed media channel.

Married and living a blissful life.

So, what this story tells us? Does it tell us to fail and be complacent? Not really, it teaches us to be strong even during the time of failure.

No failure is fatal or final. It's about giving our best and never giving up in tough situations. Good things come to those who never quit.

If you fall 1000 times; you don't become a failure, you do when you don't try to get up. Success may give you pride and pleasure, however, failure increases your success rate and experience, you learn new things from failure.

You cannot cherish success if haven't failed. Failure is proof that you're trying. Success becomes a habit if you first learn to fail.

There is a saying when you take one step towards God, he takes 10 steps towards you. If God is with you then who can be against you. If you move in life with all these positive thoughts, success is inevitable.

"Success increases your faith; however, failure makes you humble."

Moral: Success is achieved by those who never give up.

***

10 | AN OLD MAN

I was in my twenties and was strolling with my best friends on a beach.

It was an excellent gloomy Sunday, a cool breeze was simply cooler than expected, considering the humidity of Mumbai. Breathtaking scenery and a great environment with an awesome crowd. You can say, people were enjoying themselves and having a blast.

While walking on the beach, one of my friends noticed an elderly man walking and searching for something on the beach near the seashore.

He was looking perplexed and sweating profusely on a gloomy Sunday.

We thought of helping the Man. As we approached him, he said "Do not come closer", we were startled as we wanted to help an elderly man.

My friend did not like it and said: "Uncle, we just want to help you". He said "Please don't mind me", I am looking for my wedding ring and I don't want to stamp on it and push it further in the sand. We agreed and lend a helping hand. We started the search with luck and requested the old man to give up as it was getting a little darker. He said

"My wife passed away this year; however, I cannot lose her precious Ring", "that's all I care about right now".

We were searching for almost 2 hours with no luck. We thought of taking a break and then continuing the search. The Elderly man requested us to leave; however, he continued his search. When we came back, we were taken aback as the water level had increased and the old man was half immersed and still looking for the ring with his leg and sometimes with his hands.

We begged him to come out as we feared for his life. He was not ready to give up. We stood there to help him as he wasn't allowing us to enter the water. We respected his decision; however, we were vigilant about his activity.

He waved at us and requested to leave as it was getting darker and darker. We waved back and assured him that we will stick around for some time. He smiled and started again, his search.

Finally, he raised his hand and we could see a glittering metal in his hand, relief, and joy in his eyes. He came out and said, "Thank you, boys", "This wouldn't have been possible if it wasn't for you". We said, "You're welcome" with a genuine smile, he left the beach.

That day I learned the meaning of tenacity "Persistence and never giving up". An elderly man thought me a precious lesson about life. If you need something, you need to give your best and work hard and never give up.

Though he could have left the spot as his wife was no longer alive.

He worked hard to find the lost Ring after hours of a thorough search. He was persistent and did it on his own. Sometimes we need to do things on our own, be it learning new skills or achieving accolades.

Walking alone sometimes gives you the strength to protect yourself and make you mentally strong. We also have many problems in our life, don't mean we should run away from difficulties. The best solution to a problem is through it. Problems teach us precious lessons, the solution may not. People, do not run from your problems as no one will help you if you cannot help yourself. Even God helps those who help themselves.

Believe in this phrase and keep moving forward. Life is all about learning new things and testing our mettle.

"People who never give up are the bravest."

Moral: Never give up even when you have nothing to achieve.

***

11 | STUDY AT ABROAD

This story is about my elder brother – *Rajesh Kharekar*, who was always an achiever be it in sports or academics. I was always the weakest link and my parents often used to compare me to him. I always knew that I can't be like my brother. The best thing to do was to be me and learn from him whatever I could.

Back in 2008, he was working for a reputed media channel. Things were going well for him. Excellent job, Good friends and a better salary. He also started doing part-time projects to improve his earnings and hone his skill.

One fine day he came home from work and said he would like to pursue MBA in the UK, I was flabbergasted; however, I knew he would never talk anything out of the blue. The challenge was funding, yes, it was tough to get enough money for his study, especially in the UK.

He took a loan from his friends, I offered help. Also, took a personal loan at a higher rate. Finally, it was time for him to board the flight and embark on a journey to fulfil his dream. He lost his passport at the airport and on top of that, he was late to board the flight.

We searched the airport and informed the airport authority; however, in vain. He had to wait back for a month and re-apply for a passport. Finally, got his passport and flew to the UK, east London. Started his full-time MBA course, without any hiccups. He knew he had to pay his bills also pay his loan EMI. In a matter of a few weeks he was struggling to find a job and living hand to mouth.

It's sad but true that many Asian students do face racism. Things were getting bad to worse when he could not find a job. I was struggling with my bills and EMI. Things did not work as per the plan. He did not leave hope. He searched and searched, finally got a job in an IT company. Everything was falling into place and started to be on right track. When everything looked like a dream.

The whole world was struck by a severe economic downfall and a rise in the inflation rate in the year 2009. Downsizing, Zero-increment, etc. were just the common things.

My brother was still doing well with his job and study. He passed out in 2011 with flying colours and came to India with an ambition to achieve big and take care of the family.

Time passed by, he was finding it harder to get a job. He was not even hired for a BPO. I was struggling with my job and things soon turned into a nightmare when he was jobless for a year and it was time to focus and try harder.

Finally, he got a job in an IT company; however, soon it shut down due to bankruptcy. The God of fortune smiled at him once again. He got a job in Pune with almost 100% increment and he did not look back since then.

Today he is working for one of the 500 fortune companies, leading a team of engineers and earning a better salary.

You cannot expect life to be fair to you. If you do not face hardship, you cannot learn the important lessons it has to offer. No matter how hard life hits you, keep moving in the right direction and keep doing the right thing. This is a gift and a great ability of a human being.

If you have the will no mountain is too high, no ocean is too deep and no problem is too big.

"Lessons learned from the hardship is far more precious than any treasure."

Moral: Problem is a part and parcel of life, never run from it.

***

12 | NO WORK NO BREAD

I always believe in this proverb, ***"No work no bread".***

This story is about my friend - ***Pravin Nishad***. Well, I call him poo. He was just like me an average student, with a casual attitude, no ambition in life.

We became friends when I was in Sr. Kindergarten and our bond grew stronger and stronger as time passed. He left the school after completing his 3rd standard. There was a gap of 2-3 years in his schooling days due to financial conditions.

His uncle used to visit him and his sister once in six months with 2 packets of biscuits. You might be thinking, what an awful Parents' day. Trust me, life was hell for all the boarding guys, especially for him. His mom was in the United States, all the money that was sent for his studies was not spent on him.

Things got very complicated when he left the boarding school. He got caught up with bad companies; however, never forgot about us. My brother and I were his inspiration and would have given anything to be with us. He had an extremely bad experience with people and he used to say, "Life is tough outside", "I am lucky to have survived so far".

He continued his studies and completed his S.S.C. And it was time for him to join the labour force and earn money for his living. His mom was trying for him to get into the United States. Soon things got better for him, he was selected to work for a reputed media channel. He started taking things seriously and was doing well for a while. Soon he received a visa to fly to the United States.

He was in seventh heaven. He landed in the United States and started learning the tricks of the trade. His mom was running an antique boutique shop for a living and whatever money she used to earn, she would send to her daughters.

The moment you think, everything is going well; you're struck by a surprise lightning

The business was slowing down and started incurring losses due to a drop in dollar value. This not only affected him but also many people.

He started doing three part-time jobs. Call Centre, cyber cafe, and photography. He was dabbling with his work. Soon he yielded the benefit of it and sold his shop. He bought a flat in Mumbai and paid it in full. Got married to a girl he was in love with and helped to set up the business for her in States.

There is a saying "There is a woman behind every successful man". I agree to disagree, I agree that her mom called him to the US; however, he is a self-made man. Today he is living a successful life. He is not even a graduate or MBA. All I know is he is a strong-willed man and a fighter, who never gave up, but stood his ground and kept moving forward.

When I see him, I see a person who is down to earth, sincere, honest, and simple in his thoughts. The struggle has not only taught him about the importance of life but also brought the best out of him. He was not cut out for mediocre jobs, but he did it with pride as no work is small or big; our deeds are.

"You hold the key to your happiness, if you cannot unlock the mystery, no one else will."

Moral: Self-belief can cure any doubts.

***

13 | WORK ETHIC

Work is worship is an adage and few follow it like a holy book.

This story is about a person who I met in the year 2016, while I was looking to buy a flat in Mumbai. As usual, I was browsing through a website and I found a consultant who deals in real estate.

I called him on his mobile phone, however, it was engaged and hence I disconnected it. Two minutes later, I received a call from the same number, I was surprised and he introduced himself as Christopher. I told him that I am looking for a flat in Mumbai and whether he can help me with the minimum brokerage. Also, informed him that I will be going to a place somewhere in Mumbai with another consultant. He asked me about the area and I told him. He said, "Sir, please do not waste your time by visiting such a place". "It's illegal and does not fall prey to such traps."

I thought, he was advising me just because he doesn't want to lose a customer. He said, "It's alright if you do not wish to deal with me"; however, do not go to that area. I liked his word, he was willing to risk a customer and yet determined to protect me from unforeseen circumstances.

I was impressed and visited him during the weekend. He showed all A1 flats, though I couldn't afford a few. He suggested a few plans; however, due to my low salary and my brother's bad Cibil record, we could not book any flats.

It wasn't entirely my brother's fault; banks did not do justice to ensure proper payment, which led to bad credit history.

After a year with a better increment, we applied gain through Christopher. He was more than willing to help us and did not give up on us. Even though we told him that we cannot pay the hefty brokerage amount. He agreed and showed me a nice flat in 2017, my brother liked it and we started the home loan process. He was right there throughout the process until we got possession of the flat.

Today, I have a home to live in because of this man. Who did not help just for the sake of money; however, for the sake of a promise that he had made when we met the first time.

I always believe money can be earned; however, it takes years to build trust.

I took a leap of faith to trust him. He proved his honesty by sticking to his promise by never giving up on us. Honesty led to loyalty and loyalty turned into a friendship. He is a good friend and an achiever, though he has many guys working under him, he always ensures that he is with us whenever we need him.

 He is a true professional and an honest person. He an epitome of a truthful person, who gives his cent per cent at work by showing his clients the right path.

 He has his own real estate business and doing well in his field.

 An honest person, not only respects himself but also respects God and his creation.

 "A truthful person always shines like a star no matter where he is."

Moral: Be honest because what goes around comes around.

***

14 | EMPTY POTS

This story is about my office colleague who was the coolest guy I have ever known.

Thorough professional, calm, animated, and quick-witted.

He had an amazing tolerance level. He was often antagonized for his simplicity; however, never noticed him speaking with rancour.

One day, I asked him, "How can you keep calm to such remarks", "people often tease you". "Why don't you teach them a lesson?". He said, "if you cannot say something nice then you shouldn't say it at all". "People may be rude and may not treat you well, this doesn't mean you will drop down to their level and fight". "I do not feel bad for me, I feel bad for them as they're not learning anything".

He said, "when I started working in MNC", "my demeanour changed from good to bad and from bad to worst". "This was due to a lot of pressure at work and huge expectations from my family".

One day my mom and dad came to my room and said: "Beta, we have been noticing you for quite some time". "You've changed". "You look morose and stodgy". I said,

"Yes, Dad and Mom, I feel the pressure of work and family".

"I always think, about whether I'll be able to meet your expectation or not". "My dad dropped a pot, it cracked with a noise". I was startled and said, "Don't worry dad, I will clean it". He said, "Empty pots always make noise", "it means, if your mind is empty, it will make noise.

Tension, hate, low morale, past baggage can make noise in your brain and disturb you from within. You need to fill it with peace, positivity, prayers, and love to attain wisdom".

"Do not worry about things you cannot change. There is always tomorrow, that's why God has gifted us a short-term memory to forget about the past. You keep doing what you do best and leave the rest to God".

"He will guide you and help you to achieve your jails. Having a self-belief, self-belief will induce positive vibes, and this will, in turn, make you an optimist. It's difficult to break a mentally strong person".

"Well, that was enough for me to understand what he meant. Now I do not get angry or worried".

I thought about it and wondered, how on earth such people exist. You need a little anger in you to survive in this

49

world. Lesson learned and started practicing this philosophy of life.

Meeting people from various cultures and background is important as you always get an opportunity to learn something new every day. Learning new things is one of my virtues and each one of us must inculcate this habit and pass it to the next generation. As good things should always be passed on and bad things should be destroyed.

So, free your mind from bad habits, hate, negativity, jealousy, revenge and fill it with compassion, Love, Honesty, Friendship, prayer, and positive energy.

At the end of the day, you get in return what you give to others.

It's all in the mind and if your mind is filled with positive things it will silence the noise of hate and all negative things, which can keep you from the most amazing things in life.

"Always be positive and turn the negative situations to your advantage."

Moral: A calm mind is far better than an intelligent mind.

***

15 | WOUNDED PIGEON

Once I was leaning out of my house balcony, I saw a bird bathing tub in my neighbourhood. His balcony used to be flocked with pigeons and sparrows.

It was an amazing view; however, turns into a nightmare early in the morning due to their winnowing sound.

We consider the bird's bathing tub as an altruistic act and hence never complained about it. Of course, bird watching is an outstanding habit, especially when they look so mesmerizing. In addition, the tub acts as a coolant for the birds from the scorching sun.

While admiring nature's beauty, my eye caught a pigeon who was bleeding from one of its eyes. It was drinking water from the tub; however, was not washing it. It kept repeating the same act all over again. I was wondering, why the bird doesn't wash the wound. I realized that most of these birds use the tub for bathing and quenching their thirst and hence it did not wash the wound as that would have contaminated the water.

I was astonished by that act as the bird was in need and could go blind if it doesn't wash the wound. I immediately informed my neighbour to help the bird. Since all the birds were friendly with the neighbour, he got hold of the pigeon and cleaned his wound. It was not critical as the bird was not bleeding from its eye, but from the cut above the eye that it received during the fight.

Finally, the bird took flight and was looking elegant. We breathe a sigh of relief and he thanked me for pointing out that incident to me.

I appreciated him for the kind gesture as he was going against society to help the birds. It was remarkable. He said, "I am doing my bit".

The act of the bird made me realize that it was not selfish, it knew how important water is for all the thirsty birds out there.

It was a ray of hope to rejuvenate them every single day and how hard it's to find water nowadays, especially in the city.

The bird made a sacrifice by not washing its wound in the water tub and that's the greatest sacrifice I have ever seen, it could have died of infection.

Our life is also like a bird, the moment we're wounded we tend to heal it by hook or by crook. We become selfish, self-centered, and partial towards on-self. We may even hurt others to survive, that's what some of us think life is all about.

My dear friends, this bird taught an important lesson about life.

It taught us to be kind, selfless, caring, loving and taking the responsibility for the surrounding we live in. Often we misuse our rights, freedom and seldom help the needy and poor. Society needs us to spread positive vibes and set an example for others to follow. This will not happen in a day. Good things take time; however, you should take a single step to tread on the right path.

You cannot expect life to be fair to you just because you're nice to others. However, the law of karma still shines upon you if you do good to others without expecting anything in return. The purpose of life is to love one another, help one another and cherish the memory as no one is permanent. We all have to leave this world one day for the next generation to take this legacy forward.

"Happy are those who know the meaning of life and the importance of sharing it with others."

Moral: Helping others is the greatest altruistic act in the eyes of God.

***

16 | A SPECIAL CHILD

This story is about a special child who has hearing and speech impairments. She was hired by my company during a CSR activity. The purpose of hiring such special people was to create job opportunities for them and train them to live their lives independently. Encourage, motivate them; and hone their skills for a better career.

One of the girls was hired for an IT department as she was a teacher and a talented developer. It took some time for her to gel with people. Once she was accustomed to the IT culture. We learned a few things from her and she from us. The sign language, lip movement was her strength and we learned all these skills from her. Things started becoming interesting with time.

She was jovial, confident, self-dependent, humble, decent, and very caring. She was always actively involved in the team activities and never once we felt that she was a special child. She used to do an excellent job at work and was everyone's favourite.

She used to always set an example, such as reporting to an office in time and completing her within the timeline. It's quite amazing to see her achievements. People who lack nothing sometimes take things for granted, whereas special people do better than normal people.

I still remember her last working day in the company and she looked morose, sad, and pale. She wanted to continue; however, her contract had expired. She gave an amazing speech, well I was translating it for the associates.

She said, "I never felt so special", "until, she joined the company and made friends with IT associates". "I was treated like a colleague and not a special child".

"It's a great feeling when someone treats you equally and as a part of the family". "I was on cloud9 when people invited me to a dinner, sponsored snacks, offered tea and coffee". "Though, I love coffee". "I am lucky to have joined this company and team". "I can never thank you enough".

"God bless and help you achieve greater heights". She cried a bit before leaving the company. I asked her "Why are you crying"? She said, "I am not crying because I am leaving this place, but because I will never get back this moment, the best time I had with you guys".

Her speech made me realize that we do so many bad things to people unknowingly. We lie and backbite, discourage, disrespect people, and never treat people equally. The ego is just a common word in this modern world. People do have them unknowingly.

We do not appreciate if someone does better than us, someone smarter, stronger, and happier than us. Why can we just let it go? Be happy with whatever we have, so many people do not have what we do. Thousands of people have no food, clothes, or shelter. We should appreciate what we have and thank God for this beautiful life.

You should thank him for giving us the gift of wisdom, knowledge, understanding, the power to think, and Love. Why can't you stand for the weak, lend a helping hand to the needy, give food to the poor and touch the lives of people in your society? Charity begins at home and it moves from home to society and from society to the nation.

If each one of us inculcates the same ideology, then no one will ever go hungry. No one will be called poor, no one will be without shelter.

Always do "One Act of random kindness". This will not only help the needy; however, will bless you abundantly.

You should always believe in the proverb, what goes around comes around. Helping others will always make you feel proud of yourself.

"You don't have to count your blessings daily, trust in the almighty and keep doing the right thing."

Moral: Be content with all the senses God has gifted you, for some, it's a farfetched dream.

***

17 | AN ORPHAN BOY

The word "Orphan" itself sounds so lonely and scares us the most. Just imagine, you have no one to look after you except yourself. No way we can ever imagine that even in our dreams. Orphan is such a sad and harsh word, it completely removes you from society. People may even show pity and some might even disrespect you as you have no one to stand up for you.

This story is about my friend when I was in a boarding school back in the year 1989. There was a boy, who was very mischievous, rude, arrogant, and often used to get into fights. I guess he loved it. He was quite confident and outgoing and never shied from fights.

He was conscientious at work and study and never intimidated by anyone in the boarding school. I used to wonder, how come such a boy be so fearless. I never liked his attitude as he was rude, arrogant, and mannerless. I and my brother were new in the boarding and we were getting acclimatized to the environment and rules to be safe than sorry.

One day, he picked up a fight with my brother and it got ugly as my elder brother was a hot-tempered guy. He was beaten so bad that he could not walk. I would not blame him as my brother had warned him several times. Sometimes you have to fight to protect yourself.

My brother enquired about an orphan guy and that's when he came to know that he was an orphan, his dad had left him 1 year ago and no one ever visited him. He had no family and no one to share his feelings and guide him. Our hearts sank and my brother felt very bad for beating him. He wouldn't have fought had he known about the orphan boy. We knew what it was like to be an orphan as I was raised by a single parent.

We thought of doing something for him and cease the fire of revenge, which would have taken him nowhere. We used to have parents visiting day every Sunday. However, he was not so lucky. He used to sit alone on the staircase, hoping against hope to see his dad at least once.

On the visiting day, when all the boys were enjoying the company of their parents, he was sitting with a gloomy face on the staircase. We ignored him as we never wanted to show that we pity him. It's not a great feeling when someone pities you. We would rather accept if people ignore us.

When my mother left the boarding school. My brother thought of a great idea. He kept sweets under the pillow of the orphan boy and left.

We kept doing this without telling anyone. After a month, the orphan boy approached us and smiled. We smiled back at him. He said, "Thank you, no one ever cared for me as you have".

We were flabbergasted and asked, "what did we do?" He said, "Thank you for sharing the sweets with me every Sunday". "This is the nicest gesture, I have ever seen". Someone saw us keeping the sweets under his pillow and informed him. He became our best friend; however, he calls us brothers. Unknowingly, we did something which not only made him a better person but also made him feel the importance of friends and family.

We've been friends for the past 28 years and counting. Today he is working for a fortune 500 hundred company. He is independent, living his life to the fullest. People do change for good, all they need little push to follow and walk on the righteous path. You're never alone, God has his way to help you, motivate you, and make you believe in yourself. So, never feel that you're alone in this world. Find God in every human being and you'll never miss him.

"Love is all you need; the rest will follow."

Moral: God will always open a new door if you keep your faith in him.

***

18 | A GOA TRIP

The best gift you can give to your friend is honesty, enemy – forgiveness, Wife - loyalty; and family - Love. Vacations and trips do teach some life lessons. This story is about one of my friends, he was travelling to Goa, while he was occupying his seat an elderly man requested him to switch the place he wanted to see the view. My friend was not surprised as he was anyways going to doze off. He gladly offered his seat to an elderly man.

The plane arrived at the Goa airport, and he came out after security clearance. He wanted to travel to one of the famous cities in Goa; however, he could not find a cab. While he was waiting for a cab, one of the vehicles stopped near him. An elderly man lowered his car window and offered a lift.

My friend said, "You don't have to do this". He said, "this is the least I can do". "You offered me a window seat, it was very kind of you". Not a problem, he said, "we're even now".

After reaching the destination, my friend said, "bye and thank you" and went on his way. He arrived at one of the restaurants in the evening with his friends.

The restaurant was near the beach and the ambience was amazing. People were enjoying themselves.

They enjoyed their dinner and when the time came to pay the bill, everyone was chipping in with their contribution; however, when the bill arrived. My friend looked at the bill and smiled. It was written, "You're always welcome in this restaurant". The elderly were waving from the counter, he was the owner of that restaurant.

My friend said, "How can I repay you", he said, "just keep helping others", and keep the same attitude". He thanked him once again and left the restaurant. He narrated this to me while I was in Mumbai.

I did not believe him at first; however, when he showed me the restaurant bill on which it was written: "You're always welcome in this restaurant". I had to believe him. It was nice to see how few people react to the kind gestures. He was exceptional, no one helps another person twice unless they're friends. It was quite amazing to see a stranger helping another stranger without asking anything in return.

They both teach us one thing, they survived by helping one another. Sharing the seat and journey at the end of the day, it was a win-win situation. When you help others, you not only help them but also earn a blessing from God.

There is a saying that an act of kindness is so great in the eyes of God that he cannot repay it even with the whole universe. It's always good to see people helping one another and this should be an incessant act.

Many people do not talk to strangers; however, always help others if they need it. That's what life is all about. Let go of your old habit and stop being pompous. Nobody can cajole you into doing something that you do not wish to. Have faith and keep doing the right things, not for name, fame, or blessing, but because you're a nice person. It takes one person to lead by example.

So, be positive, and when you see someone in trouble help them.

That's what humans do.

"We all need help from someone or the other. You will gain only if you invest in good things."

Moral: Be helpful, that shows your attitude and respect towards others.

***

19 | CONCENTRATION

This was back in 2007, I used to commute by train to work. The memory is still fresh in my mind and it's safely stored for me to recall whenever I am down and out.

I was travelling to work early in the morning, the training was crowded, as usual, with less space; however, people were trying their best to accommodate everyone. Since I was early, I got a window seat and a school student was sitting just opposite me, I saw his book and analyzed that he was a 9th standard student. He was memorizing while travelling on a crowded train.

I smiled at him and he smiled back at me. I asked, "How can you study in such chaos". "People are shouting and some are fighting and you seem to be concentrating on your study". "How do you do it"? "How can you concentrate on your study"? He said, my Mother sells vegetables in the market and he used to help her Mom on the weekends; however, her mom never used to allow him to help her as she was more concerned about his studies.

He used to open his book in the market and study while his mom does the selling, and that's how he could concentrate on a crowded train.

He said, "Brother, you can study anywhere if you have the will and you're focused on one thing, no fish market or crowded training can shake your concentration".

It used to bother me a lot, but as time passed by, I got used to it. Now, I don't feel a thing. I can easily concentrate on my studies and I always get first class. He was poor and could not afford tuition classes to prepare for the tough subjects. Yet he was determined to do well in his studies. He wanted to be a scientist, I smiled and said, "work hard and you will get there". "Make your parents proud", "sure," he said. I got down at the station and went on my way to the office.

I was thinking about that boy and was mesmerized by his thoughts and ambitions. He was focused at a very young age and was galloping towards success. I felt very happy for the boy and promised myself that I can survive without complaining if things are not going well. I will put my head down work hard, focus, concentrate on the goal and push for success.

If I am determined to do something good, no crowd can shake my concentration. No problem can defeat me, for my will is stronger than anything else on this planet.

The boy has left a message of pearl with his sweet smile that your goal should be big doesn't matter whether you're small or big. Concentration willpower and your mettle will take you where you want to be. Life throws challenges every day and every day you have to rise and shine, thank God for giving you another day to fight and show your mettle to the world.

 All the students and people who're out there, please remember how you got through where you're right now before calling it a quit. Hard work has no substitute. No Goal is too big for you to achieve If you do not give up. If you do not try you wouldn't know how far you can run, sometimes you have to run before you can even walk. All these attributes will not only make you a strong person but will also help you lead people who need you the most.

 Remember all these things will not only keep you focused in life, but will also help you to overcome hurdles and save you from precarious situations.

"Do not bow down to problems instead face them with a smile and the right attitude. Dream Big, concentrate, and focus on the goal."

Moral: Mental strength is superior to physical strength. No one can stop you if you have both.

***

20 | THREE PILLARS

Three pillars were narrated to me by my mother when I was very little.

I had come home from boarding for a vacation. As usual, I was very excited to play with my friends and spend some time outside the home.

While playing I got into a fight and it got ugly. Parents from both sides started fighting, my mother took control of the situation and apologized, though it was not my fault.

She dragged me into the house, I was very angry and said "Mom, it was his mistake not mine". She said, "Rakesh, please sit down, calm down, and listen". I sat down and my mom said, "There three are pillars that support humans". Prayer, Love, and Humility.

"How come"? I asked. My mom smiled and said, "Prayer".

Always start your day with prayer, God is everywhere, and hence thank him.

Your day may not always be great, you may have odd days, but always remember, God works mysteriously and has his way to help people and fulfilling their wishes. The day things don't work according to your plan, just keep in mind that tomorrow is another, another sunshine, new opportunity, and new challenges and the best thing about it are you'll be well prepared. "What should I do if I have an off day"? I asked.

"Assume that God has given your best day to someone else who needed the most", she said.

Love – "I love you; however, I love God the most". She also said I am obligated to love my family, friends, and animals. It's the greatest gift of God and no one can deny it. We should love others as much as we love ourselves. God loves us and he doesn't differentiate between rich and poor, lower-caste and upper-caste. He only sees conscience and deeds. The path we choose and who we choose to become.

Love is everywhere, so as God and whoever had love in his heart, God Lives in him. "Alright! What's the meaning of Humility"? And how can I achieve it"? My mother smiles and said, "Humility can be developed with time and it's difficult to achieve". If you can master it, then you have achieved your Goal and understood life".

"Sorry mom did not understand", I said. She smiled at me and said, "You may not understand it now; however, I will go ahead and explain it to you". You will understand the real meaning when getting older". I was getting more and more eager to listen and understand the real meaning of humility that's when my Dad called my mom and asked, "Where is my bag"? It's kept on the table" and Why can't you take care of it yourself?" Mom said it in a loud voice. My dad looked at my mom and smiled and then left for his office.

"Did you see that?" My mom asked. "Yes, I did, I answered. "Dad doesn't back answer you". She laughed and said, "no, that's the epitome of humility. Your dad could have shouted at me and blamed me; however, he kept his cool and smiled at me. That shows his attitude and that's Humility".

"No matter how angry or depressed you're, never raise your voice, be humble and it doesn't cost a penny. An empty mind is a devil's workshop and an Angry mind is a devil's paradise. Don't let the devil dwell in your mind. Generate good thoughts and give anger a break, Life will be meaningful".

"All these three pillars will make you complete you if you inculcate and imbibe good habits. Now, I have passed on this knowledge to as I was by my mother. You're obligated to pass on this knowledge to your family, friends, and society".

This was an amazing example and I can never forget it. Truly, life becomes meaningful when you follow these simple rules.

"Prayer, Love, and Humility not only make you sublime but also completes you."

Moral: Strengthening these pillars will make your life beautiful.

***

21 | PEOPLE MANAGEMENT

I have left this blank so you can write/provide the story about yourself if have the Management skill or about someone who is a true leader.

It's hard to find a leader nowadays. Most leaders have integrity issues.

Moral: We all are born leaders, you just have to be yourself. A leader creates more leaders, not followers.

***

22 | TEACHER

One-word Teacher takes us back to our schooling days. It's a reminisce of our childhood. Teachers are known by their different names, such as Professor, Trainer, Mentor, leader, and so on. Teachers are often compared to God.

I too had a trainer, with time he became a mentor and a good friend. Tilak was a great honcho, a good leader, and had the potential to identify future leaders. As usual, I was working and he was a new hire and needed some help with his laptop. Being an IT professional, it was my responsibility to assist him. I requested him to give us some time so I can arrange an engineer to assist, he gladly agreed and left the IT Hub. He looked humble with a great smile, polite, and a good listener. The moment he left, I asked my friend, "Who is he"? My colleague replied,

"Tilak, Six Sigma - Master Black Belt Certified"

I liked the reply as I always wanted to learn Six Sigma. I was fortunate to be selected for a Six Sigma In-house Training, which was organized for the employees. To my amazement, the trainer was Tilak, he started with his introduction and then motivational videos. He went on to explain the importance of Six Sigma in an organization. How a company can make savings, reduce costs, optimize resources and eradicate waste.

The training was fruitful, my perception of Six Sigma and Tilak completely changed. Post-training, he instructed us to work on projects to reduce costs and was solely leading the team. I was the weakest I had no clue about PowerPoint and Excel. I still managed to prepare something to present it. He said, "It's good", you can do better and provided his input.

While working on the project I honed my Excel and PowerPoint skill and was able to complete the project in no time. He knew my challenges and hence he used to visit me and provide his input though he could have called just instructed me to visit him. He was always on his toes to help and address our queries.

Whenever I used to approach him with a problem, he used to give me three solutions and used to advise me to use my grey cells and be unique.

We all used to admire him for his thoughts, innovative ideas and -

Interpersonal skill. One day, he called me in his cabin and said, "You talk less; however, you always deliver". Always remember, "You need to work on your Interpersonal skill". "Good interpersonal skills are a prerequisite to easily get along with people and get the work done". "If you can master it, nobody can stop you".

"It will also help you lead a team and motivate others to excel in their domains".

It's been an amazing feeling to be around him. All I can say is, I was fortunate to find a mentor and a good friend like Tilak, who brought the best out of me and made me a positive human being. Teachers are a boon to society who not only guide you to achieve your goals but also make you the best person you can ever be.

A teacher is someone who knows our strengths and weaknesses and yet nature us and brings out the best in us. They do not differentiate between weak and strong, rich or poor, wise or imbecile. According to a teacher, each child is innocent, and all are unique and have special abilities to cope with studies and life. There is a saying there are no bad or good students.

The Teacher has the ability to touch the lives of millions so his/her lessons can be passed on from one generation to the next generation.

A bad teacher can brainwash an intelligent student; however, a good teacher doesn't have to try hard to teach everyone, he /she inculcates good manners and habits among his/her students and disciples through his/her teachings and actions. A good teacher gives you the freedom to express yourself and shows you the path to enlightenment.

"The teacher is the second name of a God, you're lucky if you find one."

Moral: If you have the will, you can master any skills.

***

23 | A LAWYER

Every profession has its pros and cons. Some may have a few pros and more cons and vice-versa. Ever thought of any profession, which you desperately needed; but, were not qualified to practice? Yes, I am sure we all think of something; however, life has its way of tricking us into becoming something else, the situation changes so does the profession.

This is a true story about my friend, who too had to face quite many rejections before choosing to be a lawyer. He was a hard-working guy, benign, chivalrous, and intelligent. He wanted to be an Aeronautical Engineer; things did not work for him as he had planned. He tried all the possible professions one after another, he kept failing.

Time passed by and the pressure of adopting professions became challenging for him. The peer and family pressure were getting hold of him and denting his spirit. He was crestfallen and had no clue where to begin from.

The God of fortune wasn't smiling at him. He felt like giving up.

One fine day, when he thought of giving up his hunt for a better profession and looking for whatever profession he can get hold of to get going. He found an old book, which his Dad used to often read. He started reading it as a Novel without knowing that he was reading a Lawbook. The more he read, the more interested he became in learning the court cases. From that moment, he decided to pursue Law and become a lawyer. He knew, he failed miserably while pursuing his dreams. He was determined this time to keep his focus and keep the hope alive in his heart.

 His family supported him, he excelled in his exams and went on to become a lawyer, not an ordinary lawyer, but a Criminal lawyer. No lawyer is ordinary, it requires sheer dedication and constant preparation before and after hearings. It's not easy as it may seem. He did not give up and he is reaping the benefits now. He has won many cases and has done exceptionally well.

He inspires others with his work ethic and dedication.

I believe that his life was predestined to become a Lawyer.

He failed miserably at other professions as life was pushing him to achieve something big. All this while when was rejected, he was being pushed towards his goal and his dream. He could have easily given up; however, he chose to try again and that's the true hallmark of a fighter.

So, what did we take away from this story? Never give up and never leave hope. Things will work out in your favour, if you're determined, focused, and believe in yourself. No profession is tough, if you have the will, you will achieve the impossible. Your responsibility doesn't end when you achieve your dream, it begins.

You justify your profession by being honest with your work and with the people who trust you. An honest person always carries his honour in his heart and leaves the ego at home.

Love your profession, the work you do, and inspire people around you. Remember, it takes one step to begin the journey. You may face roadblocks; however, it's the way of life to test your mettle. Keep working hard and you will reach where you're supposed to be.

Choose what you love, do what is right and create your path. Challenges are the bonus points, it trains you and prepares you for the future.

Life without challenge is like a garden of roses, without thorns. Doesn't matter what life throws at you, keep the right attitude, wear a beautiful smile, hold your head high with pride and face the problems with a humble heart.

"If you have 100 reasons to give up, think of the 1000 reasons to never give up."

Moral: Profession shows a glimpse of your work, but the character is the mirror of your soul.

***

24 | PENGUIN LOVE

Researchers have compared many animals with humans because of lots of common habits and interests. Some arguable questions about the fact; however, science has proved in their research that we both do have something in common, which makes them think like humans.

Doesn't that sound interesting? One such animal is a Penguin. It's a flightless seabird, mostly found in the southern hemisphere. They have wings; however, they cannot fly, they use them as flippers to swim underwater to catch their prey.

Just like humans, they too have a love story, they do fall in love, they too find their soulmate and stick with their mate for life. Well, humans may not stick with one partner forever, whatever may be the reasons.

When it comes to expressing love, nobody can outclass the Penguin.

When they find the love of their life, they spend their time near the sea-bed and hunt for the most attractive and round pebble. It keeps going with his search until it finds an attractive pebble. It then places it near the Penguin to decide, if the female penguin likes it, they will stick together as a couple forever.

Doesn't that sound like a movie? Yes, it does. The most amazing part of this behaviour is that they never shy away from their love, they freely express it.

This only shows an altruistic act of Love, passion, and loyalty.

I wish, only if humans can imbibe such magnificent abilities to express their thoughts freely, free from rancour, ego, imperious, and negativity. How often do we fail to express ourselves, appreciate something or someone?

Can we not live in harmony and live a peaceful life just like Penguins?

We're social and have been gifted to think, react, make decisions and most of all take control of the lives of animals, birds, and the environment.

Penguins teach us many important qualities; we humans have forgotten the ever-changing conditions of the planet. We hold the key to changing the ecosystem, the lives of all the species on this planet. Just like penguins, we too can live together in harmony and live a blissful life.

Love has no boundary so does hate, you have to choose what can harness the power to lead the people and spread the message of love, peace, and prosperity. It takes time to start something good, but once you start it, it becomes great and powerful. You don't need the nerves of steel to embark on a journey to make this earth a better place to live in.

There are 3 types of people, one who let things be as it is. Second, he/she doesn't expand his/her role beyond his/her family. Third, who embarks on this journey and doesn't stop until he finds another person who can carry on his/her legacy. It doesn't require any special skill to do something good for the people and animals of this planet.

So, you decide, who you want to be? You want to be a first, second, or third person. I wish I can say, I wish I was a Penguin, but I cannot as I can do more than a penguin can in its lifetime.

Follow these simple rules of life and you'll never regret them.

If you love someone, say it. Need help, ask for it. Want to be rich, work hard.

All these rules are simple to follow and put into practice for you to excel in everything you do one day.

Dear readers, this motivational story is an eye-opener for all of us.

Take care of yourself, your family, society, the city, state, country, and finally the environment. We live on this planet called Earth, making it a better place for your children and family to live in harmony.

We all have obligations to justify our actions to God one day, you better take the initiative to do something good for this planet.

Moral: Love everyone irrespective of their differences, that's life.

***

25 | THE POWER OF LIGHT

Once my grandfather asked me how quickly would you get rid of the darkness from the house. I answered, "I'll turn on the lights", he said, "yes, but will that fill the house with hope, the warmth of love, and positive energy?". "Don't know", I said.

My grandfather smiled and said. "You place a lamp in the center of the house, its light will spread and conquer the darkness, the lamp that's placed shows your love for the family and its light spreads the positive energy".

I understood what he meant to say; however, I continued to ask him questions. Why do we have to place a lamp in the center of the house?" "when we have so many tube lights on the ceiling." He laughed and said, "The purpose of this example is to convey consequential information about the role of an individual in the family". "Every member plays a vital role in the family".

"Father acts as a head of the family, Mother holds the family together.

Together they build a house on the foundation of Love, the roof of trust, walls of honesty, transparency, and a ray of hope for a better tomorrow.

The father and mother act as a lamp when they're together, they're strong and shine brighter like a lamp. The love for each other creates a positive energy that fills the house with the warmth of their love, compassion, personal attachment, and affection".

He made me realize that someday, I too will have a family and I should start leading a life of a gentleman, the sooner the better, and prepare myself in advance. The role I play will not only define me but will also set the foundation for my family and friends.

How often do we miss out on significant advice from our elders?

I am glad I was lucky to receive such important lessons about life from my Grandfather. He used to tell me that the stick I hold is not to support my spine; however, to show society that I am still the leader of the pack. I may not have strength due to old age, but I still have a sense of youthful exuberance.

He always believed that everything on this planet has something to teach us, we just need to find out. Every living and non-living thing has something to teach us and enlighten our path at every single step.

He also said that he has lived long enough to see the changes; however, I should never forget the good values given by our ancestors. If you find any loophole or rigid custom, you do what's right and this will make you stand out from the crowd.

Everyone requires motivation at every stage, if you're motivated, you can motivate others and keep passing the good habit to your family and friends, so they too can pass it on to their family and friends and so on.

I may not be around forever, if you really want to do something for me, do something for others and I would think that I have fulfilled my purpose. He passed away after a couple of months, but he gave away the most precious and important message of life and I always cherish his memory and thank him from the core of my heart for the person I am today.

"We all have a purpose and a significant role to play in this life. The sooner you know your role the better or else play a role that can be remembered for years to come."

Moral: Never run behind materialistic things to find happiness, find it within yourself and you will find the purpose of life.

***

9 781980 249740